A MECHANISTIC VIEW OF WAR
AND PEACE

THE MACMILLAN COMPANY
NEW YORK · BOSTON · CHICAGO · DALLAS
ATLANTA · SAN FRANCISCO

MACMILLAN & CO., LIMITED
LONDON · BOMBAY · CALCUTTA
MELBOURNE

THE MACMILLAN CO. OF CANADA, LTD.
TORONTO

From the Illustrated London News

THE ESTABLISHMENT OF ACTION PATTERNS OF WAR

The Sussex Man — The most ancient known inhabitant of England. Reconstructed from the jaw and a portion of the skull of a skeleton found by Mr. Charles Dawson in Uckfield, Sussex, England, in 1912.

A MECHANISTIC VIEW
OF WAR AND PEACE

BY

GEORGE W. CRILE

EDITED BY
AMY F. ROWLAND

ILLUSTRATED

New York
THE MACMILLAN COMPANY
1915

Norwood Press
J. S. Cushing Co. — Berwick & Smith Co.
Norwood, Mass., U.S.A.

TO

MARGARET

PREFACE

THE clinical observation of the behavior of man in injury and disease, under anesthesia and the influence of drugs, together with experimental studies of certain problems bearing upon human relations, have led me unconsciously to reach the conclusion of many scientists that man and other animals are physico-chemical mechanisms.

The data accumulated during many years of study and experimental research have become so numerous and are so well explained on a mechanistic basis that a monograph bearing upon this subject is now in process of publication.

When, therefore, through the generosity of Samuel Mather, Esq., the opportunity to take charge of a hospital unit of the American Ambulance in France was offered, it was embraced all the more eagerly since thus it became possible to study the behavior of man when under the influence of the strongest emotional and physical stress — man at war.

The substance of the following pages was written in the war zone, and, at the invitation of President Thwing, was given in a lecture at the Western Reserve University.

I lay no claim to any special knowledge of government, of philosophy, of psychology, of religion, or of the science of war — nor am I actuated by either ethical or political motives. I offer only an interpretation of the phenomena presented by man at war, from the viewpoint presented in the forthcoming volume, — " Man — An Adaptive Mechanism."

I wish to express my indebtedness to H. M. Hanna, Esq., for his generous contribution for laboratory research, and to Professor Tuffier, Dr. Alexis Carrel, Dr. Du Bouchet, and Dr. Gros, who gave me much valuable information and the opportunity of making closer observations of the behavior of man at war than would otherwise have been possible.

GEORGE W. CRILE.

CLEVELAND, OHIO,
August 13, 1915.

CONTENTS

LIST OF ILLUSTRATIONS

CHAPTER I

INTRODUCTION

A MECHANISTIC VIEW OF WAR AND PEACE

CHAPTER I

INTRODUCTION

As surgeon in charge of the Lakeside Unit of Western Reserve University in the service of the American Ambulance at Neuilly-sur-Seine I had the opportunity of obtaining the viewpoints of men who had participated in the present combat.

Visiting the front, I observed the behavior of men in the act of making war. I studied non-combatants at home, refugees, and prisoners of war, and sought similar information from reliable sources as to other nations at war.

As I reflected upon the intensive application of man to war in cold, rain, and mud; in rivers, canals, and lakes; under ground, in the air, and under the sea; infected with vermin, covered with scabs, adding the stench of his own filthy body to that of his decomposing comrades; hairy, begrimed, bedraggled, yet with unflagging zeal striving eagerly to kill his fellows; and as I felt within myself the mystical urge of the sound of great cannon I realized that war is a normal state of man.

In taking into account the training and the education of the men now at war it is obvious that although this war was precipitated by certain nations, its fundamental cause is to be found in no one nation alone; for every nation, race, or tribe has waged war. The impulse to war is stronger than the desire to live; it is stronger than the fear of death. Those who believe that man is a mechanism evolved through an endless struggle for existence, and that the struggle among men differs only in kind and not in principle from the struggle among other animals or from the equally fierce struggle among plants, will turn for the explanation of war among men to the principles of evolution. In this volume an attempt is made to see to what extent the cause and the phenomena of war may be explained on this conception. The inner processes accompanying the gross behavior of man at war I have interpreted in the light of researches long prosecuted in my laboratory, and I have attempted to correlate these apparently widely separated protocols into a working hypothesis.

I do not believe that war can be eliminated from the web of life. It is not certain that its complete elimination would be an ultimate advantage to man. My aim is to make an analysis of war; to point out the probability that these phenomena are explainable on a mechanistic basis; to seek its origin and inherent force in man; and to suggest means by which the very forces which have made cycles of war inevitable may be utilized for the evolution of longer and more secure cycles of peace.

CHAPTER II

THE PHENOMENA OF WAR

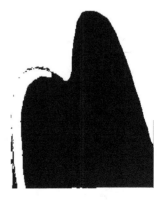

CHAPTER II

THE PHENOMENA OF WAR

Integration of the Community and the Individual for War

THE inhabitants of the warring countries are divided into three classes — those who are killing man; those who are saving man; and those who, inactive, wait at home for the return from the front. Railways are hauling food, ammunition, and men to the battle line, and hauling back the wounded. Factories are turning out uniforms and guns, powder and shot. Telegraphs and telephones speak only of war. The printing press describes battles, and records the names of the dead. Hotels and schools are hospitals, and parks are drilling grounds. Iron and steel, copper and lead, are implements of injury and death; while the universities and scientific laboratories are deserted sanctuaries. Wealth and station, titles and honors, are lost. Man, stripped of his trappings of civilization, has reverted to a common brute level.

At the different military hospitals, bankers, business men, artists, and noblemen are orderlies; college men, great hunters, and soldiers of fortune drive ambulances; artists, authors, actresses, and social leaders are auxiliary nurses. A luxury-loving, self-indulgent class have been born again. They have found the pleasure of making a bed, giving an alcohol bath, and repairing an automobile; of submitting to discipline and of conquering a daily task; they have felt the deep though unexpected satisfaction of sacrifice and service; they have met and merited the grateful eye and have heard the appreciative word earned by their useful work. These are among the good by-products of war.

On the other hand, the slippered grandfather has been drawn from the fireside to the plow; the younger son and daughter from the school to the factory. Old age has been robbed of its serenity, youth of its opportunity, while the burying squad has marked with a rude cross the resting place of the masters in science, art, and industry, and the daughters of the land have the scant comfort of the memory of a soldier's death.

The first effect of the declaration of war was the mobilization of the forces within the body of

"THE BURYING SQUAD HAS MARKED WITH A RUDE CROSS THE RESTING PLACE OF THE MASTERS IN SCIENCE, ART AND INDUSTRY, AND THE DAUGHTERS OF THE LAND HAVE THE SCANT COMFORT OF THE MEMORY OF A SOLDIER'S DEATH."

each individual in the warring countries. In other words, the *kinetic system* [1] of each individual was activated. There was an increased output of adrenalin, of thyreoiodin, of glycogen; and an increased mobilization of the Nissl substance in the brain-cells, from all of which there resulted an increased transformation of energy in the form of heat, motion, or chemical action. The individual moved quickly; he sang or prayed; his face was flushed; his heart beat faster; his respiration was quickened and there was usually an increase in his body temperature. Fight gained possession of the final common path; it dispossessed the routine activations of peaceful occupation and human relations. In each individual the organs and tissues of his body mobilized their stores of energy just as each government mobilized its resources of men and material. The people of every nation petitioned God to help them kill their neighbors. Millions of wives and mothers prayed to God to help no one, but to restrain all from killing. But God remained neutral. Prayers availed nothing. The action

[1] The kinetic system is the group of organs in the body by means of which man and animals transform the potential energy contained in food into muscular action, emotion, body heat; in short, it is the system by whose activity life is expressed. It may be compared to the motor of an automobile.

patterns of war had become established in the brains of the men of the nations.

During the period of peace each country had accumulated much surplus wealth, surplus men, surplus confidence. Conscious of its existing strength each was confident of victory. In this confidence the supreme stimulation to fight against his distant enemy so mobilized the energy of the soldier that in the absence of the object of his attack he used this mobilized energy in song. Two general types of motor acts are produced by the mobilization of energy for fighting a distant enemy; namely, marching and singing. Why not laughter or weeping?[1] Weeping means defeat, and the realization of defeat comes only after the battle. Laughter is the result of a sudden release of energy, mobilized to accomplish some definite muscular action. If the enemy should surrender unexpectedly before he was attacked, then there would be laughter on the part of his conquerors. Marching toward the enemy and singing are the two types of muscular action fabricated by the kinetic system when the activation for fight is dominant. But the mother or the wife, in whom the dominant stimulus is the desire

[1] The Origin and Nature of the Emotions.

to retain the son or the husband at home, weeps because the parting for her means defeat. During the season of mobilization, then, the kinetic activation of the people is expressed by marching and singing on the part of those going to battle, and by silence or weeping by those left at home. The kinetic systems of those who fight and of those who remain at home are abnormally active; but, in the first stage at least, the activating substances thrown into the blood are more completely utilized by the muscular activity of the marching and singing husband than by the still and sobbing wife. The kinetic systems of the soldiers during mobilization are less strained than are the kinetic systems of those he left behind.

The activation of the soldier in the presence of actual danger as facing an evenly matched enemy is precisely the same as is experienced by men in many other situations in life, — in the first encounter with big game; in being held up by a burglar; in a railway accident; or in facing a serious surgical operation; although most of all the activation of battle resembles the hunting of formidable wild beasts.

Man in war, as a hunting animal, is elusive, resourceful, adaptive, brave, and persistent. When hunted, man turns hunter himself, and like wolves men hunt in packs. Therefore when men are mutually hunting each other their brains are intensely activated to this end, and all other relations of life are dispossessed.

Trench Fighting

The nearer the trenches, the more desperate and intense is the fighting. In trench fighting both sides have adopted every variety of flame, acid, and explosive that ingenuity can devise. Every ruse, every stratagem, is employed in the close personal contact. It is as if one were contending all day and all night with a murderer in one's own house.

Under these conditions the personalities of the men become altered; they become fatalists and think no longer of their personal affairs, their friends, or their homes. Their intensified attention is directed solely to their hostile *vis-à-vis*. They look neither to the right, to the left, nor behind. The gaze of each is fixed upon the end of the hostile gun, which may hold for him — his future!

To indicate the fierceness of the struggle in the Argonne, I know of one instance in which an officer who had been wounded on the "hell-strip," "No-

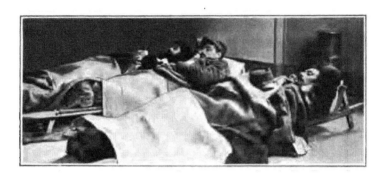

WOUNDED SOLDIERS FROM THE TRENCHES IN THE ADMITTING ROOM AT THE
AMERICAN AMBULANCE

Man's Land," that red lane between the German
and the French advance trenches, lay there for six and
one-half days, then died.   Neither rescue nor capture
was permitted.   Flashlights played over this wounded
man at night, and food was thrown to him from the
trenches by day.   Dead bodies lie on this strip or
dangle on barbed wires for days and weeks and
months.   ꞏ ɩꞏ

In the first impact of war many men in all of the
armies became insane; many underwent nervous
breakdown; some became hysterical; but the great
majority became seasoned and maintained a state of
good health.   The rigid, alert, muscular response
uses up much energy; the appetite is active, diges-
tion good, and if the supply of food is adequate the
balance of nutrition is maintained.   I have observed,
however, that soldiers in the trenches show unusual
lines of strain upon their faces, giving them the
appearance of being from five to ten years older
than their actual ages.

While the proximity of the trenches has brought
intensive fighting, it has also brought its counter-
part, — fraternizing between the opposing sides.
The men hear each other talk and sing, one side sig-
nals, the other answers, and their representatives

appear and exchange tobacco, food, and news-papers.

On Christmas day the son of an English friend of mine participated in a friendly interchange of greetings. The soldiers on each side agreed mutually to the cessation of hostilities, and spent the day in chatting and burying their dead. Officers ordered their men back to the trenches. The men, however, agreed that until a stated hour they would shoot into the air. When that hour arrived both sides put on the mask of war, and resumed the business of killing each other.

Soldiers have told me that they find it difficult, at times impossible, to shoot an individual enemy when they can see his face so clearly that he might again be recognized.

In general we may say that the warfare of the trenches represents an intense, though not necessarily a destructive activation of the kinetic system, which might be compared with the kinetic activation of prolonged athletic contests, or prolonged intense mental application, such as a chess contest, or the taking of difficult examinations.

Artillery Fire

In contrast to the *vis-à-vis* trench fighting with rifles and hand grenades and dynamite, artillery fire is more severe only when concentrated, and the concussive effect of bursting shells brings other forms of injury. The sudden explosion of the shell shocks the ear, frequently breaking the ear drum; it shakes the body, and often produces a molecular change in nervous tissue. The rarefaction and condensation of the air cause such violent changes in the gaseous tension in the blood as to rupture blood vessels in the central nervous system — thereby producing an injury in a vital part and causing sudden death. The process is in a measure comparable to "caisson disease" or "bends" in workmen laboring under atmospheric pressure in tunnels under water. But artillery fire is less personal than the rifle or bayonet. The artillery man rarely sees the object of his fire; he has no personal contact with the enemy, but suddenly finds himself under a scorching fire, from a source which he cannot ascertain, from an enemy he cannot see. It is like quarreling by telegraph.

In describing an important artillery engagement,

c

an observer told me that although there were a large number of guns in action he could not see a gun nor did he see a man. The general and his staff were stationed behind a small mound, where a telephone kept them in touch with the action at the front. The scene was silent and grave. Now and again a messenger came and went, and a small stream of wounded soldiers were seen walking slowly back. At one moment a soldier who had shown especial bravery in capturing a *mitrailleuse* was sent to the general, who shook his hand and congratulated him. Only by telephone were these onlookers finally apprized that the battle was over and that a victory had been won. Following the wounded soldiers one could note a progressive change in their condition. They became weaker and more nervous and as the stimulus of battle faded, the relaxation and fatigue became manifest. This battle was in the woods of the Vosges. The same observer described another battle on an open plain in which, although the entire field was in sight, not a man nor a gun could be seen, so complete was the obliteration. Aside from the sound of the firing of heavy guns and the whistle of shells not a sight, not a sound, gave evidence that in the plain a battle was raging.

Waiting under Fire

Lying under fire for the first time while waiting
for orders to charge is perhaps the most trying
ordeal for the soldier, for his instinct urges him
to face the on-coming enemy. He realizes the possibility of immediate death. His kinetic system is
speeded to the utmost. He is activated for a fierce
physical attack. He is under extreme emotion.
His heart pounds loudly against his ribs, his hands
tremble, his knees shake, his body is flushed with
heat, he is drenched with sweat. In mechanistic
terms the phenomena manifested by the soldier
waiting under fire may be interpreted as follows:
His brain is activated by the approach of the
enemy. The activated brain in turn stimulates the
adrenals, the thyroid, the liver. In consequence
thyreoiodin, adrenalin, and glycogen are thrown
into the blood in more than normal quantities.
These activating substances are for the purpose of
facilitating attack or escape. As the secretions thus
mobilized are utilized in neither attack nor escape,
heat and the muscular actions of shaking and trem-
bling are produced. The rapid transformation of
energy causes a correspondingly rapid production

of acid by-products. These increased acid by-products stimulate the respiratory center to greater activity to eliminate the carbonic acid gas. The increased adrenalin output mobilizes the circulation in the limbs; withdraws blood from the abdominal area; causes increased heart action and dilatation of the pupils. In addition, the increased acidity causes increased sweating, increased thirst, and increased urinary output, all of these water phenomena being adaptations for the neutralization of acidity.

Thus the intense activation of the soldier waiting under fire for orders is explained on mechanistic grounds, and the resultant changes in the brain, the adrenals, and the liver are easily demonstrable. It is this strong stimulation of the kinetic system to fight or to flight that in the first experience sometimes results in fleeing. The subsequent stimulus is never so intense as the primary stimulus, and with experience the kinetic system is progressively less driven, until at last the soldier is said to be 'steady under fire.'

The Charge

Soldiers say that they find relief in any muscular action; but the supreme bliss of forgetfulness is

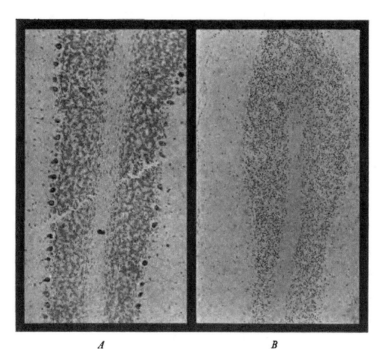

A *B*

SECTION OF NORMAL CEREBELLUM SECTION OF CEREBELLUM AFTER INSOMNIA
(× 100) — 100 HOURS (× 100)

Compare the well-stained clearly defined Purkinje cells along the margin of section *A* with the faint traces of the Purkinje cells which are barely visible along the margins of section *B*.

than his savage progenitors, is thrilled by the death agony of his fellows. The action patterns of ontogeny seem but shallow tracings upon the deep grooves of phylogeny; in the cultivated man of to-day is the beast of the phylogenetic yesterday.

The Retreat — Fatigue — Loss of Sleep

Perhaps one of the greatest retreats in history was that of the allied armies from Mons to the Marne. Again and again I listened to the story from men who participated in that retreat and their personal experiences varied but little.

After a sustained and heavy action at Mons, being overpowered by the enemy, the allied armies began the retirement which continued for nine days and nights. One hundred and eighty miles of marching without making camp is the story of that great retreat in which the pace was set by the enemy. Only rarely were sufficiently long halts made for the men to catch a few moments of rest. Food and water were scarce and were irregularly supplied.

The point of paramount interest in that retreat is found in the sleep phenomena experienced by these men. It has been shown that animals subjected to the most favorable conditions, kept from

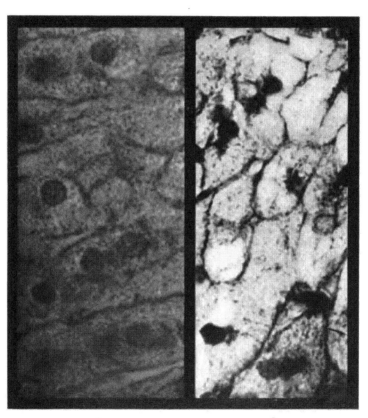

A

SECTION OF NORMAL ADRENAL
(× 1640)

B

SECTION OF ADRENAL AFTER INSOMNIA
— 100 HOURS. (× 1640)

Compare *A* and *B*, noting in the latter the disappearance of cytoplasm, the loss of some
nuclei, and the generally disorganized appearance of the cells.

exertion or worry, supplied with plenty of food, and in good hygienic surroundings, do not survive longer than from five to eight days without sleep. The mere maintenance of the conscious state is at the expense of the brain, the adrenals, and the liver, and these changes are identical with the changes in these organs wrought by exertion, infection, and emotion. The changes wrought by these activators *can be repaired only during sleep. Sleep, therefore, is as essential as food and air.* In this retreat from Mons to the Marne we have an extraordinary human experiment, in which several hundred thousand men secured little sleep during nine days, and in addition made forced marches and fought one of the greatest battles in history.

How then did these men survive nine days apparently without opportunity for sleep? They did an extraordinary thing,—they slept while they marched! Sheer fatigue slowed down their pace to a rate that would permit them to sleep while walking. When they halted they fell asleep. They slept in water, and on rough ground, when suffering the pangs of hunger and of thirst, and even when severely wounded. They cared not for capture, not even for death, if only they could sleep.

The unvaried testimony of the soldiers was that every one at times slept on the march. They passed through villages asleep. When sleep deepened and they began to reel, they were wakened by comrades. They slept in water, on stones, in brush, or in the middle of the road as if they had suddenly fallen in death. With the ever on-coming lines of the enemy, no man was safe who dropped out of the ranks, for no matter on what pretext he fell out, sleep conquered him. Asleep, many were captured. That the artillery men slept on horseback was evidenced by the fact that *every man lost his cap.*

The complete exhaustion of the men in this retreat from Mons to the Marne is vividly told by Dr. Gros of the American Ambulance, who with others went to the battlefield of the Marne to collect the wounded. On their way to Meaux they met many troops fleeing, all hurriedly glancing back, looking more like hunted animals than men, intent only on reaching a haven of safety.

When the ambulances arrived at Meaux at midnight they found the town in utter darkness. Not a sound was heard in the street, not a light was seen. The only living things were hundreds of cats. They called, they shouted, in vain they tried to

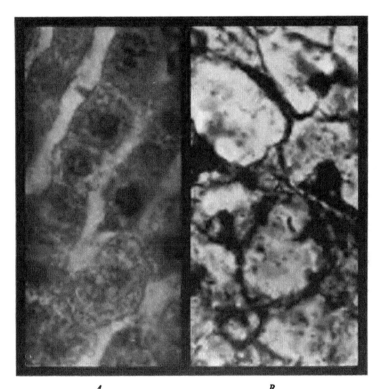

A

SECTION OF NORMAL LIVER
(× 1640)

B

SECTION OF LIVER AFTER INSOMNIA
— 100 HOURS (× 1640)

Compare *A* and *B*, noting the vacuolated spaces and general loss of cytoplasm in the latter.

arouse some one. At last they succeeded in awakening the mayor, to whom they said: "Can you tell us in what village we will find the wounded? We were told there were many here." The mayor replied: "My village is full of wounded. I will show you." With the aid of a flickering lamp, they threaded their way through dark streets to a dilapidated school building. Not a light! Not a sound! There was the stillness of death! They rapped louder, there was no response! Pushing open the door, they found the building packed with wounded — over five hundred — with all kinds of wounds. Some were dying, some dead, but every one was in deep sleep. Bleeding, yet asleep; legs shattered, yet asleep; abdomen and chest torn wide open, yet asleep. They were lying on the hard floor or on bits of straw. Not a groan, not a motion, not a complaint — only sleep!

Surgical aid, the prospect of being taken to a good hospital, the thought of food and drink, of being removed from the range of the enemies' guns, awakened no interest. There was a sleepy indifference to everything in life. They had reached the stage of unconditional exhaustion, and desired only to be left alone.

Dr. Gros' ambulance corps took the worst cases first. These were soldiers with shattered legs and arms, some with compound fractures, some with penetrating wounds of the abdomen and chest. They made little or no complaint on being picked up, placed in ambulances, and transported. The only sound they uttered was when the torn flesh, glued to the floor by dried blood, was pulled loose.

Thus these men, goaded by shot and shell, and the ever-advancing army; for nine days without adequate sleep or food; in constant fear of capture, and finally wounded, — thus these men, more dead than alive, came to the hospital: and thus they slept on while their wounds were dressed.

After deep sleep for two or three days, during which they wanted neither food nor drink, they began to be conscious of their surroundings: they asked questions; they experienced pain; they had discomforts and wants; — they had returned from the abysmal oblivion of sleep.

That these men had conquered the overwhelming impulse to sleep sufficiently to continue marching and fighting during that nine days' retreat testifies to the dominating power of battle. That a soldier falls asleep during the dressing of severe wounds

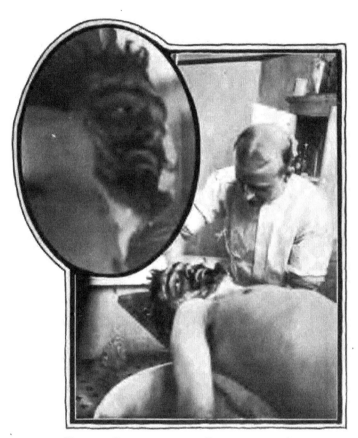

WOUNDED SOLDIER FROM THE TRENCHES UPON ADMISSION TO
THE AMBULANCE. NOTE THE FACIES OF EXHAUSTION.

tells a trenchant story of the intensity of the stimulus that kept him awake. The exhausted, half-dead appearance of these soldiers was usually transformed by one long seance of sleep during which the brain, the adrenals, and the liver had in some measure overcome their physical exhaustion.

Dreams

The harmony of the sleep of the exhausted soldier has but one discordant note, and that is the dream of battle. The dream is always the same, always of the enemy. It is never a pleasant pastoral dream, or a dream of home, but a dream of the charge, of the bursting shell, of the bayonet thrust! Again and again in camp and in hospital wards, in spite of the great desire to sleep, a desire so great that the dressing of a compound fracture would not be felt, men sprang up with a battle cry, and reached for their rifles, the dream outcry startling their comrades, whose thresholds were excessively low to the stimuli of attack.

In the hospital wards, battle nightmares were common, and severely wounded men would often spring out of their beds. An unexpected analogy to this battle nightmare was found in the anesthetic dreams. Precisely the same battle nightmare, that occurred in sleep, occurred when soldiers were going under or coming out of anesthesia, when they would often struggle valiantly, — for the anesthetic dream like the sleep dream related not to a home scene, not to some dominating activation of peaceful days, but always to the enemy, and usually to a surprise attack.

One day a French soldier, in the first stage of anesthesia, broke the stillness of the operating room, transfixing every one, while in low, beautiful tones, and with intense feeling, he sang the Marseillaise.

Pain

Pain as a phenomenon of war exhibits several variations of great interest, the key to which is found in the conception of pain as a part of an adaptive muscular action. Identical injuries inflicted under varying conditions yield pain of unequal intensity. The most striking phenomenon exhibited by soldiers is the absence of pain under the following conditions : (a) In the midst of a furious charge the soldier feels no pain if wounded ; and sore and bleeding feet are unnoticed. In the overwhelming excitement of battle he may be shot, stabbed, or crushed without

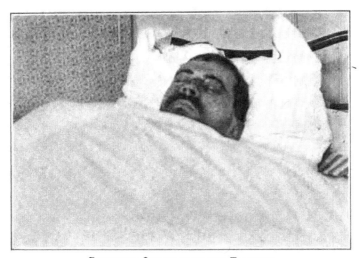

EXHAUSTED SOLDIER FROM THE TRENCHES

This man slept continuously for two days and nights after admission to the American Ambulance.

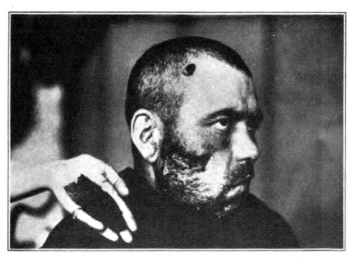

SHRAPNEL WOUND OF JAW

The piece of shrapnel removed from the wound is held by the nurse.

feeling pain. (*b*) The blow of a high velocity bullet or projectile unaccompanied by the heat of battle causes no pain on impact, though there may be a burning sensation at the point of entrance, and the soldier may feel as if he had been jarred or struck. Frequently he first learns of his wound from a comrade. (*c*) In the state of complete exhaustion in which loss of sleep is the chief factor pain is quite abolished. (*d*) Under heavy emotion pain is greatly diminished, even prevented.

We can now offer a mechanistic explanation of these exceptions to the general rule that bodily injury causes pain. During the overwhelming activation in a charge, the stimulus of the sight of the enemy is so intense that no other stimulus can obtain possession of the final common path of the brain — the path of action. We have elsewhere shown [1] that pain is inevitably associated with muscular action; therefore if a bullet or bayonet wound is inflicted at the moment when this injury cannot obtain possession of the final common path, it can excite no muscular action and consequently no pain. Hunters attacked by wild beasts (Livingstone) testify to the fact that the tear-

[1] The Origin and Nature of the Emotions.

ing of the flesh by claws and teeth cannot dispossess the excessive activation of the brain by the realization of danger. For this reason the teeth and claws of the beast do not cause any adaptive muscular response and therefore there is no pain. In like manner the emotion of fear in the soldier holds possession of the final common path so that muscular action against local flesh injuries is prevented. Not only in war does emotion overcome pain; so does great anger; so does the exaltation of religious fanatics in their emotional rites.

An explanation of the fact that even when other stimuli do not possess the final common path a rifle ball may pass through the body without causing pain is found in the postulate that the sense organs react only to those stimuli in the environment to which they have become adapted and to those stimuli only when they are applied within the limits of adaptation. Too bright a light blinds; too loud a sound deafens. There is no receptive mechanism adapted to the stimuli of the X-ray. The high-speed bullet is a recent development, and even were it not recent, no muscular action could have availed as a defense against it. The force of its impact and its

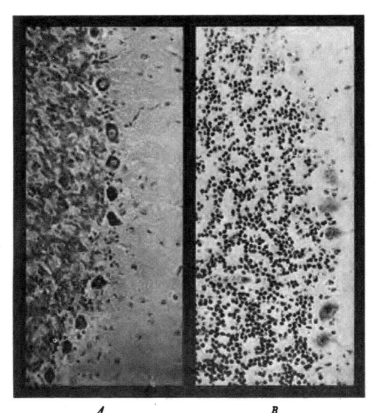

A	B
Section of Normal Cerebellum (× 310)	Section of Cerebellum Showing Effect of Extreme Physical Exertion (× 310)

speed is beyond the range of muscular adaptation and therefore it elicits no muscular response — no pain.

As for the diminished pain in exhaustion, especially exhaustion in which loss of sleep is an important factor, the following explanation seems adequate: As we have stated already, pain is always associated with muscular action. Therefore if the kinetic system is so completely exhausted that no more muscular action can be excited, pain is impossible. In a state of exhaustion, therefore, unless the injury is sufficient to mobilize the dregs of energy remaining in the kinetic organs there will be no muscular action and no pain. This explanation is strongly supported by the fact that as soon as exhausted soldiers had slept long enough to restore in some measure the energy of the brain, the adrenals, and the liver, then muscular action and coincidentally pain were evoked normally.

We know also that in a state of exhaustion, much less anesthesia is required to confer freedom from pain than is required in a normal unfatigued condition. A remarkable example of the depression of pain in the presence of other more dominant stimuli is the case of a young British sergeant, who in a severe engagement while standing near a battery had his leg partially cut off by a shell that failed to explode. He felt no pain, merely a jar, and discovered his injury only when his leg failed to support him. He hopped to a near-by stack of grain and lay down behind it. Here he took out his dull one-bladed knife and completed the amputation, feeling no pain in making the division. An ambulance squad started for him but immediately the enemy fired upon them, killing one. The fire becoming more intense, the sergeant rolled over and over into a near-by ravine. The enemy advanced so fast, that in his excitement he struggled up and forgetting that his leg was gone threw his weight on the stump. Even then he felt no pain. For several hours he lay there without pain until after the danger had passed and he was removed by the stretcher squad. Then pain took possession of the final common path and his suffering began.

The fact that pain is an accompaniment of muscular action and that without some associated muscular action there is no pain, makes it clear that there can be no pain when the system is as exhausted as in the soldiers in their retreat to the Marne. A striking illustration of the absence of pain in the presence of extreme fear and exhaustion is found in an incident

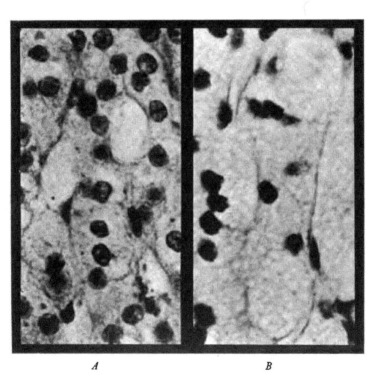

A

SECTION OF NORMAL ADRENAL
(× 1640)

B

SECTION OF ADRENAL SHOWING EFFECT
OF EXTREME PHYSICAL EXERTION
(× 1640)

related by Dr. Gros, which occurred during the transportation of wounded soldiers who had made the exhausting march from Mons to the Marne.

It was a dark night and the hospital train filled with the wounded was crossing the river Ourcq. The engineer failed to see that the bridge was broken, and the train plunged into the river beneath, some of the cars remaining on the bridge and some being suspended in mid-air. The patients in the suspended cars, struggling like worms in a bottle, were thrown in heaps against the ends. The engine exploded, the cars were filled with live steam, and many of the wounded were burned to death. The suspended cars could not be righted and the wounded were dragged out by main force.

Such intensified cruelty could not come even to trapped animals. It could come only through the ingenuity of man — through the machinery of civilization. And yet these men, suffering from fear, excessive marching, fighting, the loss of sleep, and the plunge into darkness, scalded, steamed, grilled, and finally shattered and bleeding, — these men felt no pain.

There is one other factor which prevents pain — the so-called "wind of the ball" or concussion. In the early days of the Far West this was known as creasing, and was utilized in catching wild horses. The horse was stalked to a water-hole where by a sure aim a rifle ball was sent through its neck just above the spinal column. The "wind of the ball" knocked the horse down and it could easily be roped. Thus in war man knocks down many of his fellows by the "wind of the ball." A ball grazes the head or the neck, and the soldier falls. A ball or shell in passing through the arm or leg grazes a nerve trunk and there is sensory and motor paralysis below it. A ball passes through the spinal column, and the entire body and extremities below are paralyzed. There are cases also in which the pain sense has been lost although apparently no injury has been received, the anesthetic condition being analogous to hysterical anesthesia. For these I can offer no interpretation.

Courage

That animals accept battle at sight and struggle unto death excites no comment. That the herbivora secure their daily food bravely under the eyes of their enemies is taken for granted. We expect even the worm to turn. Fighting to the death has been

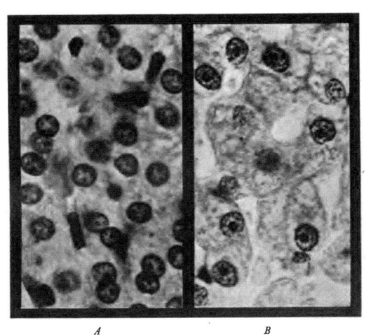

A

SECTION OF NORMAL LIVER
(× 1640)

B

SECTION OF LIVER SHOWING EFFECT OF
EXTREME PHYSICAL EXERTION (× 1640)

the game of life among the progenitors of man.
In the evolution of man the strongest and the brav-
est have survived. Thus bravery is an evolved
phenomenon and as such must have survival value.
The soldiers of all nations at war are brave and all
die as bravely as animals die.

The Wounded

Usually the wounded are not rescued until night —
they are left to make a lone struggle until darkness
protects them. This is not because it is undesirable
to rescue them during the day, but impossible!
Even at night the rescue work is hazardous, as shell
fire plays constantly over the field. The Red Cross
has proved as much a target as a protection, for in
this war ambulances and hospitals are fired upon.
The toll of killed and wounded surgeons in the first
weeks of the war ranked with that of the artillery
officers.

The fate of the wounded is uncertain. The
wounded soldier who will soon be able to return to
the front is kept within the sound of the guns lest
he lose his morale. Here with no sense of security
he must make his recovery. Like trapped animals
wounded soldiers often complete the amputation of

their own mangled limbs: they may be buried alive in shelled trenches; they may be frozen to death or die of hunger and thirst; they may be burned or their frozen feet may drop off with their shoes. The wounded must often consort with the dying — the dead — the decomposing. They may become ill, delirious, insane before they have reached the hospital train.

In a heavy action neither side knows just when the blow will fall; neither side knows how many will be wounded. The railways are choked with onrushing troops. There are often no means for considering the wounded, the order of military train service being—first, fresh troops; second, munitions; third, food; fourth, the wounded. How many freight cars would be needed to carry ten thousand wounded? Yet this is but an ordinary toll. In emergencies the wounded are packed into cars — freight cars, any kind of cars, on the floors of which there may perchance be straw. Under such stress it may take days for the hospital train to make even fifty miles. The dead from time to time are cast out like dead bees from a hive and the quiet moans of the occupants of these charnels are drowned by the vigorous songs of the fresh young patriots on the next

COMPOUND FRACTURE OF THE ARM WITH SERIOUS INFECTION.

Most wounds become infected, especially those made by fragments of shell, as pieces of dirty clothing are carried into the wound.

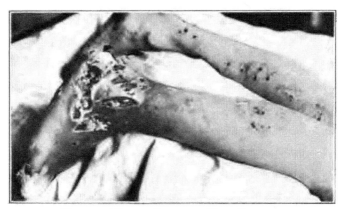

MULTIPLE WOUNDS CAUSED BY HAND GRENADE.

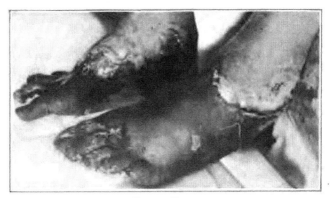

FROZEN FEET.

A frequent sequel of life in the trenches.

track eager to fling themselves into the hopper of the greedy mill which grinds steadily on while the nations applaud.

Causes of Death

At the end of the first year of the war it was estimated that ten million soldiers had been killed, wounded, or were missing.

The common causes of death are: (*a*) fragmentation of the body — a sudden, painless exit; (*b*) shock — a violent restless exit; (*c*) hemorrhage — a quiescent, fading exit; (*d*) infections — blood poisoning, gas gangrene, and tetanus. These are the wider avenues through which the soldier marches into oblivion.

The phenomena of war merely show that only in the possession of more complex reactions does the animal — man — differ from other animals. The veneer of civilization is astonishingly thin. Man argues like the brute — man fights and kills like the brute. Man dies like the brute.

Non-combatants

When a civil community is first under fire it is terrorized. In time this terror wears away and life under the sound of shells goes on quite normally. I observed that from Furnes to Ypres the farmers were quietly tilling the soil under active shell fire. In one instance just at the outskirts of Ypres I saw a fresh excavation made by a shell which had fallen on a newly made furrow. The farmer was working at one end of the furrow and the German artillery at the other end! The farmer seemed no more disturbed than the artillery. An aëroplane fight high above our heads called forth the rapt attention of every one in the fields, on the roads, and in the houses, but even so the excitement was less than one usually sees at a baseball game.

In Ypres, so long under bombardment, and so extensively battered, some of the citizens had stolen back in spite of shells and had resumed their daily routine. I recall a little plaster house at the edge of the town, in the doorway of which two women were pleasantly gossiping and two little girls were playing with dolls. The nearer the front one goes, the more quiet and serious every one seems. It is the solemn atmosphere of the consecration of human life.

The effect of war on non-combatants, especially on the women, is as characteristic as on the fighting

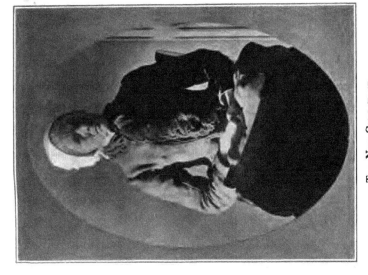

The Non-Combatant

Sergeant —— of the "Restless Fourth"

men. Species-preservation and self-preservation are often antithetical; in other words, struggle for life dispossesses impulses to procreation. As the struggle for life lessens, the phenomena of procreation increase, a fact demonstrated by the fashions, amusements, and the type of indulgences of prosperous seasons. In a period of war, however, the fittest males are called to the battle line, and the women are mobilized for relief. The antithetic reaction of saving life becomes as strongly stimulated as the reaction of destroying life, and the impulse to procreation loses its claim to the final common path. Self-indulgence disappears. The males struggle in battle for the preservation of their tribe or nation against their enemy; the females struggle in the care of the sick and wounded to preserve their race and tribe, by mitigating the destructive work of the enemy. The military unfit strive to fill the vacant places in the ranks of industry and of science. Thus the non-combatants are mobilized as completely as are the combatants.

The non-combatant, however, is more emotional than the combatant. Emotion being an activation without resultant muscular action, the non-combatant finds immense relief in physical work. The woman craves to nurse the wounded soldier, and she willingly performs for him the most menial services; the more she is driven emotionally by having sons or husband at the front, the more she is impelled to exert physical care on some soldier — any soldier, even one of the enemy, and in that work she finds her salvation, for without a working interest she would be impaired, even destroyed by the emotion of fear.

One evening while Paris was in Zeppelin darkness, I kept a professional appointment in one of a certain group of buildings. I lost my way in the great darkened structures and wandered from floor to floor, building to building, through empty halls, until at last I met an aged servant who showed me the way to the room where I found the great Metchnikoff! This building was the famous Pasteur Institute. Before the war from ninety to one hundred scientists were here engaged in research! The next day I visited the Sorbonne, whose intellectual activities of other days are now represented by a small group of military discards. No less deserted must be the famous seats of learning of Germany, Austria, Russia, and measurably of England.

The brains holding the germs of mighty truths are enriching the soil of the far-flung battle lines today, and the torch of civilization has been handed to us.

Grief

The quality of grief excited by the death of those who have fallen in battle differs from the grief for those who die in peace. In war, grief is mitigated because it is a common lot and is the result of service to the native land. Even in war, however, circumstances alter the quality of grief for the fallen. When a bridge has been saved, a hazardous message delivered, defeat averted, or the tide of battle turned, then grief becomes glorified and the death of the hero causes exhilarative pride. If, on the other hand, death is the unheroic result of fever, grief is unassuaged.

End Effects

The most striking end effect of war is race deterioration. The effect of war on the race is seen in the effect of emigration on New England. In stature, in energy, and in enterprise, the New England farmer has deteriorated by losing so many of his fittest sons. It has been stated that Napoleon shortened the stature of the French by several inches. The human animal is not unlike other animals, — no one breeds from scrub stock. This war will diminish the stature and vigor of the human race to the extent that the killed were larger and stronger than those who remained at home.

The birth rate at the end of the war will be changed. It will be increased among the victors, decreased among the vanquished. In this respect man reacts like animals. Animals breed best amidst plenty, less when food and shelter are inadequate, and least of all when harassed in captivity.

I am told by an official of a large insurance company that in Europe suicides are now increasing in the civil population and that diabetes increased after the Balkan War. I am told that among the Belgians, Bright's disease, apoplexy, diabetes, neurasthenia, and insanity increased after their vivisection by Germany. It has been estimated that the adult Belgians have lost, on the average, ten pounds in weight and have aged from five to ten years. As a whole the nations at war have sustained vast moral and mental, as well as physical injuries. They have lost the unit value of millions of years of life. The biologic aspect of the end effects of war will be considered later.

Compensations

There are certain compensations for war. War and preparation for war develop national consciousness — increase national and individual efficiency; they lead to industrial expansion, to invention; they bring order and discipline to men; they develop unselfishness and charity; they strike down needless distinctions; and through war or the threat of war the masses have often achieved personal liberty. Military training benefits the individual and the nation; it teaches obedience, respect for authority, punctuality, team play; it promotes physical development and personal hygiene. Military training is a valuable preparation for any civil career.

How much of the great advance of European civilization has been due to rivalry and struggle among the great powers it is difficult to estimate, but no such progress could have been achieved under conditions of guaranteed peace, for progress is born of struggle. But the crucial question remains: What is the impelling force that makes man wage war?

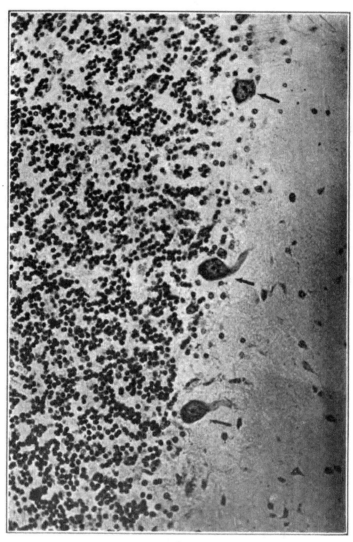

A

Section of Normal Cerebellum (× 310)

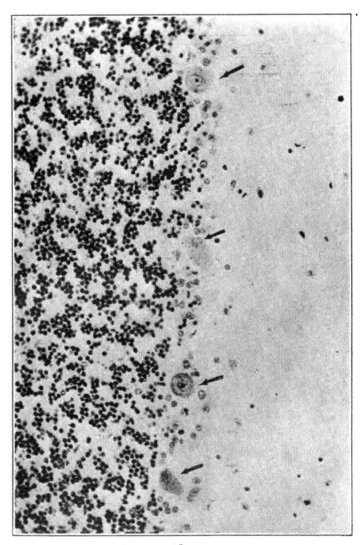

B

Section of cerebellum of a soldier who had suffered from hunger, thirst, and loss of sleep;
had made the extraordinary forced march of 180 miles from Mons to the Marne;
in the midst of the greatest battle in history was wounded by the explosion of a
shell; lay for hours waiting for help, and died from exhaustion soon after reaching
the ambulance. Compare the faded-out exhausted Purkinje cells, indicated by
arrows, with the Purkinje cells in *A*, also indicated by arrows.

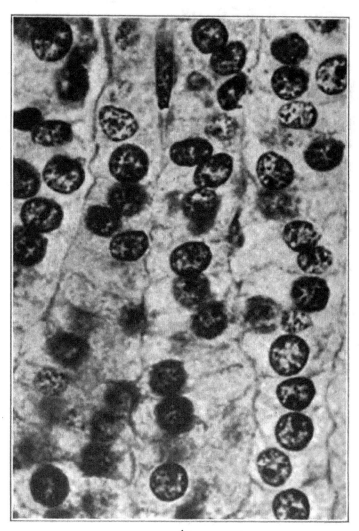

A

Section of Normal Adrenal (× 1640)

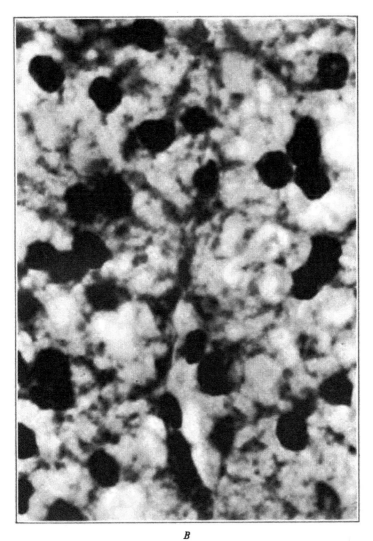

B

Section of adrenal of soldier described in preceding illustration (× 1640). The general
disintegration of the cells, loss of cytoplasm, misshapen and eccentric nuclei illustrate the effect of emotion, exhaustion, lack of sleep, pain, infection, and trauma.

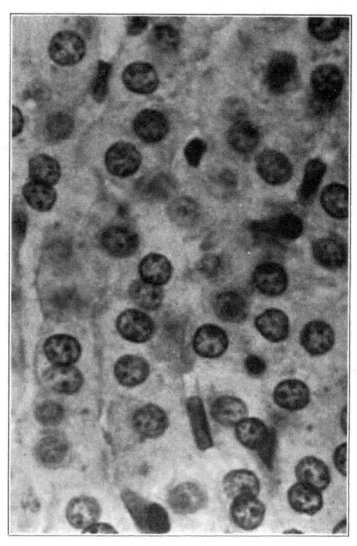

A

SECTION OF NORMAL LIVER (× 1640)

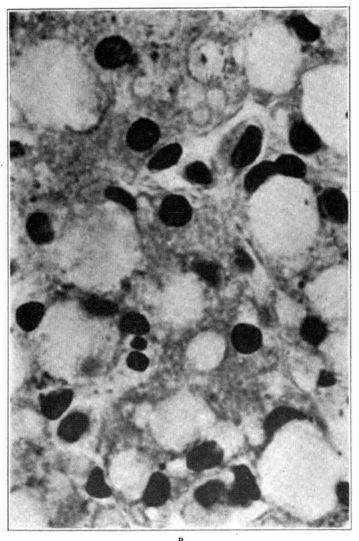

B

Section of liver of soldier described in preceding illustration (× 1640). The general disintegration of the cells, the loss of cytoplasm, and the vacuolated spaces within the cells illustrate the effect of emotion, exhaustion, lack of sleep, pain, infection, and surgical trauma.

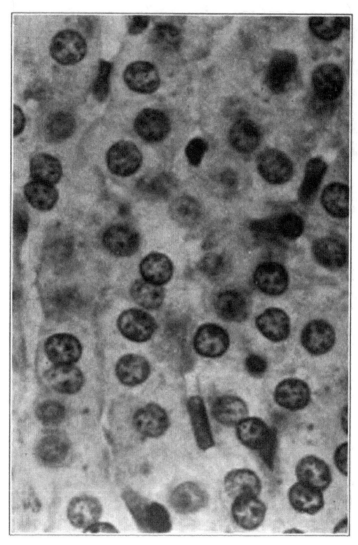

A

SECTION OF NORMAL LIVER (× 1640)

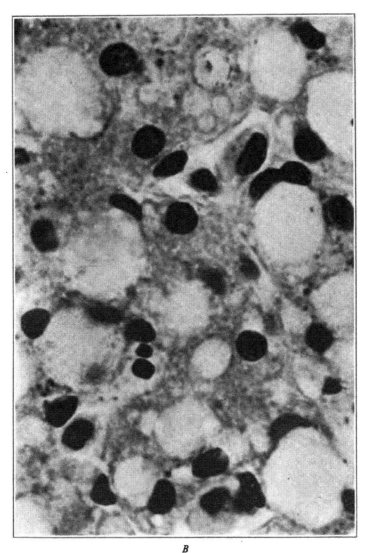

B

Section of liver of soldier described in preceding illustration (× 1640). The general disintegration of the cells, the loss of cytoplasm, and the vacuolated spaces within the cells illustrate the effect of emotion, exhaustion, lack of sleep, pain, infection, and surgical trauma.

CHAPTER III

A BIOLOGIC INTERPRETATION OF WAR

CHAPTER III

A Biologic Interpretation of War

The Rise of Man through Struggle

It is through the fortuitous mating of an infinite number of ancestors, whose characteristics have been transmitted down to the present time, that the individual of to-day has become the product of all the past.

The path of descent is the same for civilized man, half-civilized man, savage man, prehistoric man, and so on down the pathway through the long line of the successive progenitors of man, an unbroken succession from the present to the lowest forms of life. Within himself every individual holds the imperfect record of this ascent along a crimson trail. We may suppose that eons ago as a weaker creature man's distant progenitor was driven by powerful enemies to the trees where his strategy was further evolved and his fore-feet became hands. Cautiously he returned to the hostile ground of his

ancient enemies and resumed the battle by utilizing the forces of nature. He discovered fire, he
found metals, he fashioned simple tools and weapons; made dugouts; tamed animals; planted seeds,
utilizing Nature herself to aid him in obtaining food, shelter, and clothing, and in securing protection against his foes.

In the gradual evolution of man the ever-present
law of continuity holds. There is no break in the
path from the orgy of the naked savage to the sen-
sual dance of to-day; from the careless sale of a
Bushman's daughter to the fixed price of the daughter of a living Crœsus; from the savage grapple
with wild beasts to the present grinding struggle of
competition. From birth to maturity civilized man
is tossed upon the same seas of passion and wrecked
upon the same rocks as those upon which the sim-
plest tribesman was wrecked eons ago! During this
great upward struggle man has steadily gained
greater control over the forces of nature and has
become more and more completely adapted to his
environment. By the fundamental process of a
physical contest with environment he has made
the forces of nature turn with "tireless arms the
countless wheels of toil." Through breeding he

has modified the physical form and the texture of the flesh of many domestic animals; he has found ways of utilizing the sun's energy of millions of years which was stored in the immense vegetation of the carboniferous age in the form of coal; he has harnessed the waterfalls. With these vast stores of energy he has made iron and steel; with iron and steel he has encircled the globe with huge agencies of transportation that conquer time, space, and gravity, and through these agencies there are brought to him products of every land. He has devised language and the printing press, which have given him a record of the notable motor and emotional acts of his ancestors.

These descendants of the cave man have captured and domesticated lightning; they have enslaved the world with a copper nervous system which enables them to activate the action patterns of, and in turn be activated by, hundreds of millions of the human race. A slight change in the chemistry of a human brain cell may wreck a bank in India, fire the first gun in a great war, or break a woman's heart. Such is the web of life man has woven and by means of which he so completely dominates the earth.

Pursuing, escaping, and fighting, the brute adaptations, have been gradually modified during the rise of man, until now in the complicated machinery of modern life the human energy expended by the savage in pursuit and escape and fight is expended in the shop, in transporting commodities on land and sea, in preparing armaments, and in pursuing the arts and sciences.

The most powerful activator of man to-day, therefore, is his fellowman. He is at war with him in business, in education, in philosophy, in the fine arts, in the professions, in the pulpit, in politics, in winning mates! In all his waking hours and in his dreams he exerts himself against his fellows. The savage stalks or ambushes his enemy or his prey in direct personal effort and settles the issue by physical prowess; civilized man stalks, ambushes, and attacks indirectly through the media of trade and commerce. The savage settled his issue in one physical bout; indirectly through the organized community civilized man may hurl himself against his rivals with every atom of his strength for months and years, and though this civilized combat draws no blood and tears no tissue, nevertheless the indirect battle is waged to its finish in bankruptcy, want, suffering, broken health, and premature death.

The leaders of political parties, of opposing churches, of industrial and commercial corporations, individuals in medicine, law, education, literature, art, music, sports, even in philanthropy, daily wage these indirect, but no less destructive contests. In the field or in the shop the individual exerts his strength directly against his task, so that indirectly the energy he thus expends yields in return food, clothing and shelter and a modicum of pleasure for him and his family.

Thus in civilized life man is hurling his energies either directly or indirectly against his environment to the end that he may live. From the simple laborer to the head of the greatest commercial, scientific, educational, or governmental organization, the transformation of energy is made in accordance with the same principle, by the same organs, and for the same reasons as the transformation of energy in uncivilized man or in the lower animals.

In the selective struggle for existence the acquisition of food developed speed, power, cunning, and craft in all species, but as the food suitable for each species is different, each has developed special activities, and special responses to hunger. Man labors long and hard to this end, and the possibility of want is one of his great sources of fear; but a critical analysis will show that there is no difference between the orderly struggle of men to supply their material needs and the brutish attacks of the carnivora upon their prey.

The dominant, constant influence of the phylogenetic response to the instinct of self-preservation as expressed in the acquisition of food is nowhere more clearly evidenced than in the persistence of the hunting instinct in man. By stealth and strategy our progenitors caught birds, animals, and fish. They robbed birds' nests, ate fruits and cereals and nuts. At some remote period a savage Newton noted the relation between the egg and the bird, the seed and the plant, and as a result, like the ants, man learned to cultivate and modify plants and animals for his own use. Some early progenitor discovered the use of simple weapons like sticks or stones and learned how to increase their efficiency by shaping them. And then came the greatest benefactor the human race has ever known — the unknown progenitor who discovered how to make and control fire!

THE PHYLOGENETIC ORIGIN OF WAR

The protection of home and family against invasion.

Even after the discovery of these simple but efficient aids to their existence, however, the progenitors of man for a long period (geologic time) must have depended largely on hunting and fishing. That much of the hunting and fishing of prehistoric man was done by similar means to those employed by the carnivora is shown by children in their instinctive stalking of birds and small animals, and by the way in which untaught boys instinctively stalk their game in hunting. How suggestive it is that man, possessing vast fortunes and surrounded by every luxury, frequently yearns to hunt and to fish, to be dirty and hungry and wild, to stalk and to kill, caring not at all for discomfort or the flight of time — that thus easily his civilized veneer may be dispossessed by the spirit of his savage hunting progenitors. It is the savage recall. It is the savage in him that is throwing all of his resources into the task of catching and killing his prey; and when at last the salmon or the trout is hooked, what a display of excitement over the conquest! It is as if a life were at stake.

This is not strange when we recall that on innumerable occasions the life of the fisherman's progenitors must have depended upon the catching of a single fish. Those individuals who did not exert themselves sufficiently to provide food for themselves were themselves destroyed by the more industrious beasts and left no progeny. The almost universal excitement of man in the presence of wild game testifies to the tragic seriousness of the ancestral hunt. It is indeed a strong and deep savage instinct that can with ease thus dispossess the brain of business, ambition, worry and care.

As in hunting, so in play, the phylogenetic brain patterns of the species are manifest, the play of each species being as characteristic of the whole behavior of the species, as is the real life work of the adult animal. Thus hunting animals play at fight; the herbivora at escape; and strategists — monkeys and man — imitate in their games the activities of hunting, fighting, lovemaking, and rearing offspring. Play is the expression of energy set free during consciousness, running over the only nerve paths, activating the only mechanism the young animal possesses. It would be no more possible for a lamb to bite and claw like a kitten than for an automobile to imitate a threshing machine. The play of children shows their line of descent. They chase and escape; they "hide and go seek;"

they lead and direct toy animals; they construct
towers and bridges with blocks; they kiss and
embrace; they "play mother."

During the years that pass until they become
adults they play games progressively more intricate; but in all periods of life games consist of
contest; of struggle; of attack and defense. In
the playing of cards, chess, golf, billiards, tennis,
baseball, football, the spirit of fight is ever present;
fight not alone of the players, but of the spectators.
Thus sometimes we see the strictest police precau-
tions against violence on the part of the spectators
and the players in the close contests of rival teams.
Football is perhaps the most satisfying game to the
full-blooded youth, as this gives him a savage grapple
with naked hands with his fellows. Little wonder
that slugging is so hard to repress!

Man has shown his greatest ingenuity in the
means he has devised for harnessing the forces of
nature to provide his food and shelter and clothing,
and he is as jealous of the soil that produces his
food as he is of life itself. For an inch of this soil
as an individual, and as a tribe, a state, or a nation,
man is willing to kill or be killed. Line fence
quarrels are proverbially bitter and uncompromis-

ing. In the frontier, disputes as to the ownership of animals often cause quarrels and feuds totally out of proportion to the material considerations involved. In the early West the minimum punishment for horse stealing was death. All these latent passions awakened by interference with food-producing rights apparently arise as a result of the same ancient law that explains the excitation of the hunter.

In community life, however, individual rivals rarely submit their claims for ownership or supremacy to the test of physical combat, for through the evolution of law and convention the distribution of food and the furtherance of procreation may be accomplished in orderly fashion. So efficient and orderly are the means of creating, storing, and distributing food and clothing that the honest winner of more than his own share must have either some natural advantage or a greater efficiency than the average man. Nevertheless, the mere fact that one individual, community, or nation has acquired more than his average share excites a desire in those who have less to do something to hinder or prevent this material advantage.

Many civilized human beings are so admirably

adapted to the community life that they are content with their own winnings and therefore are not jealous of the greater winnings of their more favored or their more able fellows; but in many the reactions of the uncivilized man and the brute still prevail, and in consequence their reaction to the superiority of a fellow-being is to desire by any means to drag him down to their own level. In like manner all human beings who achieve something that others wish but fail to accomplish, awaken the brutish reaction of jealousy — and the jealous, like wolves, run in packs. The effect on the pack is the opposite; their time and their lesser efficiency is consumed by their futile effort to destroy a fellow whose greater efficiency is attested by their sincerest tribute — the tribute of pack pursuit. The envied leader is occupied only in cultivating the field he possesses; while the pack endeavors to destroy his preëminence. If a member of the pack falters, he himself is devoured. Jealousy, therefore, whether between individuals or nations, is an instinct of phylogenetic origin, and like the hunting and the play instincts is expressed by brutish and savage reactions.

What is the impelling force which throughout phylogeny has provoked this unending contest?

The natural increase of animals and plants is at a greater rate than their food supply — and in consequence plants and animals have ever been subjected to selective struggles. It is as a result of this continuous selective struggle that the organic world has attained its present balanced status.

Man a Mechanism

Under this conception every reaction of man in the survival struggle is inevitable and is determined by the forces employed in the struggle. It would seem, therefore, that to properly understand the inevitableness of war, man should be considered as a mechanism, whose reactions under a given set of conditions are as inevitable as are the reactions of any other mechanism, such as a locomotive, for example.

If we assume that man *is a mechanism* that acts as a machine, that is a machine like a locomotive or an automobile, it is necessary to define the device which starts his activity, and which continues, modifies, and terminates that activity. If man is such a mechanism, we should be able to show not only physical reasons why he moves, but why he fails to move as well, just as there are demonstrable physical reasons why a locomotive moves and why it fails to move. In the case of an engine the burning of a given amount of coal produces a given amount of work in the form of heat and motion; in like manner in man the consumption of a given amount of food produces a given amount of work.

We know that the brain contains the mechanism that drives the body; we know that environment drives the brain, and that environmental forces reach the brain through the mediation of the sense organs. But what is the mechanism within the brain by means of which a given stimulus causes different effects in different brains? Why will one man run away and another attack on receipt of identical stimuli? We postulate that there are in the brain of man and of the lower animals receptor mechanisms analogous to the receptor mechanism in the eye, — the rods and cones, — which like the apparatus of a wireless receiving station are attuned to receive light waves only of specific wave lengths, *i.e.* between 397 and 760 millionths of a millimeter.

Even more delicate than the light-receiving mechanism of the eye, however, are the receptor mechanisms which we assume to exist within the brain

— intricate mechanisms consisting of a vast number of parts or patterns each of which has been endowed by evolution with the quality of being modified by each passage of specific energy over it. Each passage of specific energy initiated by a given stimulus facilitates the passage of energy from an identical stimulus at a subsequent time. As a result of the passage of energy over each of these patterns, energy is released for the performance of an action specific to the exciting stimulus. It is postulated that thus are established action patterns which determine behavior, conduct, and the various human reactions.

In other words, we assume that there exist within the brain certain structures which have been evolved to receive specific energy and to transmit that specific energy to other mechanisms in the brain where energy is stored in such a labile form that it may readily be released to pass over certain nerves. As a result of the passage of energy over certain nerves certain groups of muscles are activated, and specific, adaptive acts are performed. Thus the soldier marches, halts, aims, fires, fixes his bayonet, charges, retreats. If his brain is blown off, his mechanism can no longer be activated through the senses. If it were possible, however, to stimulate the various nerves running to the muscles that participate in a given act by an electric current of the same intensity as the current of energy received from the brain, the headless soldier would march, halt, aim, fire, fix bayonet, charge, retreat; and as long as the nerve-muscle mechanism remained physiologically intact and the electric current was supplied, shot and shell could not stop him.

We assume that the mechanisms in the brain which determine the response made by an individual to any stimulus have been evolved as a result of the selective struggle of the human species.

If we contrast the large central battery — the brain — of man with the small brains of lower animals, we can see one of the mechanical differentiations of man from the lower animals.

As a result of the multiplicity of action patterns evolved in the larger brain of man, the body of man is driven in more intricate ways than that of any other animal. The life of the carnivora as a class is divided between sleep and prowling for food; of the herbivora, between feeding and rest; the survival of man, however, depends upon his versatility.

As compared with most lower animals man is continually on duty.

For this reason the organs of man are driven harder than the organs of the lower animals. How rarely do we find diabetes, neurasthenia, insanity, Bright's disease, Graves' disease, cardiovascular disease among wild animals or among the quiescent domesticated animals. The horse, whose *kinetic system* is driven by the *kinetic system* of man, who is goaded and restrained by man, has many of the diseases of man. The cow, whose yield of flesh and milk is greatest when she is best fed and least disturbed, is given a perpetual rest cure by man, and consequently with her disease is comparatively rare.

The actions of man are the result of adequate stimuli, and however indirect the stimulus or the response, the activated mechanism and the form of its response are of ancient phylogenetic origin and have been woven into the web of life. As a result of present community life, of convention, of customs, and of law, but few of the many excitations to combat are met to-day by physical combat. In such a case, if the discharge of energy from the stimulated action pattern is not expressed in muscular action, emotion results — a state which may be more dangerous to the individual even though less so to his fellow.

The destruction caused by excessive motor and emotional driving results in various diseases. Against the conditions of the stress of present-day life that produces these diseases man reacts in various ways. He is driven to hunt and to fish, to play games, to ride horseback, to go to the country, to cultivate literature, art, music, and the drama. All of these are self-preservative reactions, achieving results because they change the integration — give relief from the usual driving stimuli.

Man avoids these tense kinetic fellow-being stimuli by means of unions, combinations, trusts, protective laws, any artificial means by which he may escape the heat of battle with his fellows in his struggle for existence. In addition, man may react to these tense driving human stimuli by minimizing the activity of his motor mechanism through the use of agents that depress the activity of the brain — such as alcohol, tobacco, drugs, anesthetics; and sometimes hard driven man may plunge into oblivion through suicide.

How then does this apply to war? We shall offer evidence which tends to show that war is the end effect of the action patterns previously established in a people. Man is not a stranger to fight — the oceans would not hold the blood he has shed. The carcasses of his slain would heap the earth. Probably the entire surface of the earth has been many times slain in its organic form by man, and perhaps the organic forms he has slain in greatest numbers have been those of his own kind.

Thus through the ages has been established within the brain of man the phylogenetic action patterns of killing, equaled in their intensity not even by the phylogenetic action patterns of procreating. The action patterns of killing are the product not of phylogeny (species experience) alone, but of ontogeny (individual experience) also. The part played by ontogeny — by parents, teachers, literature, public opinion, and the fine arts — will be more fully discussed later. It is sufficient to say here that the behavior of an individual or a people, the dominant action patterns of whose brains have been formed by responses to the stimuli of killing, will be warlike, and cannot be otherwise.

Animal behavior is full of examples of action patterns of fight. Among gregarious animals the head of the herd fights rivals at sight and to a finish.

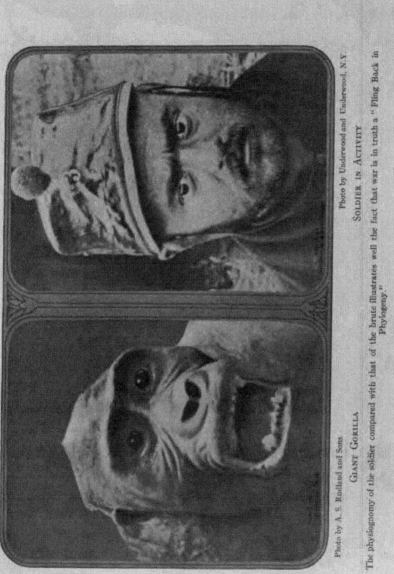

Photo by A. S. Rudland and Sons

GIANT GORILLA

Photo by Underwood and Underwood, N.Y.

SOLDIER IN ACTIVITY

The physiognomy of the soldier compared with that of the brute illustrates well the fact that war is in truth a "Fling Back in Phylogeny."

Deposed leaders do not fight each other. Man and other animals do not fight for nauseating food, nor for the possession of waste places. Human fight is waged for food, shelter, and raiment; and for mates. Obviously no action patterns could have been established for a struggle for poisonous food, for desert land, for unfit mates; for evolution tends only toward construction, never toward destruction, and evolution toward starvation or away from procreation would lead inevitably to annihilation.

In general we may say that physical contest among animals tends always toward the survival of the fittest. Whether it is a dog with a bone amidst a pack of hungry fellows; a people with fertile land; or an individual possessing a surplus of desirable necessities or who has achieved success,—the reaction in others expressed by a struggle for possession is normal and to be expected, unless it is known that the fortunate individual or people will share his or their possessions. *The individual habitually shares. Nations rarely share.*

The state has a right to a part of the possessions of the individual as taxes for the benefit of all the people. Where competition is active the possessions of one individual to-day may be won by another individual to-morrow. Each individual hopes to come into the possession of surplus wealth; but the wealth of one free nation never normally becomes the property of another free nation, except by trading or by force. One nation never bequeathes property to another; no nation has a chance of inheriting the property of another nation. No free nation pays another nation's taxes, therefore nations are more selfish than individuals. In consequence there is less attraction and more antagonism between nations than between individuals.

The war reaction of a people is the final expression of its action patterns; their conduct is natural, inevitable. They are not to be blamed; they need to be understood. Nations having no action patterns for war need no praise for their peace; they also need to be understood. War and peace can be comprehended only when they are considered as end effects of action patterns established by phylogeny and ontogeny.

CHAPTER IV

A MECHANISTIC VIEW OF GERMAN KULTUR

CHAPTER IV

A Mechanistic View of German Kultur

GERMANY to-day stands as an example of the inevitableness of action patterns. On this conception we cannot blame her, but it is essential that we understand her.

Let us suppose that at this moment Canada contained a hostile population of one hundred and seventy-five million people, a trained army of five million, and a chain of forts along the boundary. Suppose that Mexico were a rich, cultured, and brave nation of forty million with a deep-rooted grievance, and an iron curtain at its frontier. Suppose that Cuba were the richest nation in the world, and that she possessed and controlled one fifth of the earth's surface and were the undisputed mistress of the sea. Let us suppose further that these conditions had existed for forty-four years, and that during this time action patterns in the brains of the children of the United States had been formed and facilitated for the

killing of the surrounding rivals; that during this time
the United States had learned that to defend itself,
it must have efficiency and wealth, and that if the
people as a whole were to survive, they must re-
nounce their individuality, must surrender themselves
to the state, to be used by the state, for the advantage
of the people themselves.   The state being in danger,
and the head of the state being responsible; the state
would strive to its utmost to effect self-preservation.
The people of the state seeing themselves as a collec-
tive mechanism, prospering beyond their rivals,
would believe strongly in their system, and more
and more would be willing to surrender themselves
to the state, realizing that their individual labors
would be more effective when guided by the *highest
talent of the few, the supermen, than when guided by
the mediocre talent of the masses.* They would
see everywhere law and order; they would be cared
for when sick and aged; the education and training of the masses would be fostered; their nation
would each year become more secure in wealth, in
mass efficiency, in armament, in science, in security
of life.

In nature such a system as this is well known and
is equally efficient.   It is the system of ant colonies,

in which the individual ant has been evolved to re-
nounce its individual reaction for the good of the
colony, and ultimately for the good of the individual.
This is the *Kultur* of the ant — and an efficient system it is, since the ant next to man most completely
dominates the earth.

Is this a fanciful conception? It represents the
position of Germany during the past forty-four years
and now, for German *Kultur* has been made possible
only by the powerful rivals which surround her. It
was obviously against this steady hostile breeze
that the ruling class of Germany flew its military
kite, and transformed the action patterns of the
brains of sixty million people into those of renun-
ciation of individualism, and the acceptance of
collectivism. This is obviously a *Kultur*, — but can
man be made to respond to this *Kultur* in the absence
of powerful, threatening neighbors? Has the mechanism of the *Kultur* elements of danger to itself?

In the presence of a common danger, or a danger
commonly believed to exist, a danger that threatens
destruction, men and animals react along purely
self-preservative lines. It is only a real danger that
has transformed the German individual into a state
machine, has given him the "*es ist verboten*" re-

action. On this conception the action patterns and the behavior of the German seem natural and expected. His dominant action patterns are for killing and conquering his hostile neighbors and preserving himself.

That the hive and colony reaction is not an evolved instinct with the German, but that it is a production of his *ontogeny* rather than of *phylogeny*, is shown by the fact that the children of the million or more German immigrants in America are as individual as are the Americans of other stocks. They dislike *verboten* and wish to work for themselves. The war adaptation of Germany is seen in the duels among officers and students; in the uniform customs and manners of the German people; in their respect for authority in all walks of life — in industry, in science, in amusements; it is seen in the absence of national sports, sports being representations of fight. *War* is the sport of the German.

There is ample evidence to show that whether for good or ill the German has reached a new adaptation, at least an adaptation new to the present cycle of history. Perhaps in bygone days this may have been a common adaptation, but it could be made only in the presence of strong enemies.

The ultimate fate of the German *Kultur* may then be foreseen. By virtue of its sheer efficiency it has reached the point at which it feels itself equal to making a conquest of the world, and, like the Athenians, to enforcing its system on a subjugated world.

Treitschke and Nietzsche have evolved an altruism based on force, as against the altruism of Christ based on simple justice. Germany in arms today is Nietzsche's philosophy. Its advantages are startlingly obvious, but are its foundations secure? Germany will ultimately conquer or be conquered. If she is conquered, her people will believe that there is a flaw in the premises and think their sacrifice was in vain. Should Germany win and should she conquer the world, then she would lack the fundamental motive force which created *Kultur*, — her hostile neighbors. She would be a kite without a breeze, a cancer that has killed the body on which it fed.

The individual Ally begins by assuming the right of the individual; the German begins by renouncing the right of the individual and recognizes only the right of the state. The German looks upon the individual as building material, as such possessing only the rights of brick and mortar. It is the duty of the individual to surrender his individuality; 'of the superman to build without loss or obligation. In this sense to Germany the invasion of Belgium is justified, because its purpose was to further the cause of *Kultur*. The individual citizen of Belgium and the State of Belgium are isolated phenomena, while *Kultur* is a biologic principle. As Nietzsche puts it, the strong should feed on the weak and crush them when needed. The individualist opposes these views. Therefore the individualist and the *Kulturist* estimate the invasion and the crushing of Belgium from opposite points of view — each being equally sincere in his judgment.

After all, morals are only expressions of biologic states, only results of action patterns; and what are good morals from the standpoint of a wolf, are bad morals from the standpoint of a sheep.

But again the question rises: Can a people through force be given action patterns against their will? Rome never succeeded in Romanizing the world. Rome tried to subjugate Belgium; Belgium is here — Rome has passed. Napoleon failed; the Moors failed; England never assimilated the Irish nor the Scotch; Russia the Poles; nor the Manchus the Chinese. England has learned by a large experience over a considerable period of time that subject races cannot be altered by force. Germany has not succeeded in extending her doctrine of centralized force into her colonies. Force creates action patterns in opposition to, not in consonance with, that force. A people may be brutalized into formal submission; but brutal treatment results in creating in the brains of the children the strongest action patterns of opposition and of hatred. The conquering enemy can never supplant the influence of the hating mother who plants action patterns in the brains of her children when the shades are drawn.

CHAPTER V

MECHANISTIC VIEW OF THE VIVISEC-
TION OF BELGIUM

CHAPTER V

A Mechanistic View of the Vivisection of Belgium

According to the bias of the speaker or writer the vivisection of Belgium by the German army must be considered as necessary strategy or inexcusable atrocity. It is not my purpose here, however, to discuss from any viewpoint the ethics of this forceful invasion, but rather dispassionately to analyze in scientific terms its effect upon the Belgian people themselves.

German strategy required the submission of Belgium. Whether right or wrong, the purpose of Germany was to strike down the armed and the unarmed resistance of Belgium with massive and overwhelming force. To accomplish this it was necessary, first, to defeat the Belgian army; and second, to terrorize and subjugate the whole people so that both physical and moral resistance would be impossible.

Never in contact with animal life is man as cruel as when he is in destructive combat with his own kind. Though millions of domestic animals are killed annually, the death of each is relatively instantaneous; though hosts of wild animals are hunted, they are, as a rule, either killed instantaneously or, if captured, are allowed to live in an environment approximating their native haunts. Though thousands of animals are used in medical research, their sufferings are relieved by anesthesia. Moreover, in all these injuries inflicted upon animals by man, *emotion* plays a relatively unimportant part, and the effects of emotion may be greater and more far-reaching than the effects of physical violence alone. When a herd of animals is dispersed, they may easily adapt themselves to a new environment, for neither the old nor the new has been of their own creation. On the other hand, when a nation of men is dispersed they leave behind the complicated machinery of civilization in whose creation each has borne a part, and by means of which the living of each is secured. For them no new pastures wait with ready-made sustenance, but instead they must create a new web of life through which alone they may wrest from the soil their daily bread. Therefore for man, with his many reactions, with his complicated emotions, with his intricate web of

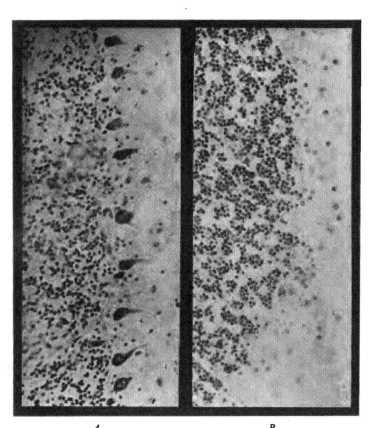

A

Section of Normal Cerebellum
(× 310)

B

Section of Cerebellum Showing
Effect of Extreme Emotion
(Fright). (× 310)

life, there are vast possibilities for crushing moral
injuries whose effects are more destructive than
the effects of physical injuries alone.

Let us consider what would be the expected result
of the intense psychic and physical activations
inflicted upon the Belgians in the light of laboratory findings, bearing in mind, however, that in
no laboratory has the activation of animals been
carried to such an extreme, or has such suffering
been inflicted as in the vivisection of Belgium.

As we have already stated, the body of man is
driven by his brain, which in turn is driven by
stimuli received from the environment through
the sense organs. As a result of the transmission
of these stimuli to the brain, a certain portion of
the energy stored in the brain is transformed, and
either muscular action or some chemical change results, the muscular action being for flight, fight, the
acquisition of food, or procreation; the chemical
reaction for the maintenance of the chemical purity
of the body.

These final responses are made possible by the
system of organs which constitutes the kinetic
system, — the brain, the adrenals, the liver, the
thyroid, and the muscles. In my laboratory it has

G

been shown that as a result of emotion — fear or anger, physical injury, exertion, as well as of many other kinds of activation, physical changes are produced in these organs and the normal potential alkalinity of the body is diminished. Clinical observations as well as the examination of the organs of patients who have died from various causes demonstrate clearly that in human beings as in animals, insomnia, physical injury, physical exertion, fear, anger, grief, homesickness — any intense emotion — produce physical lesions in the organs of the kinetic system.

When the brain is overwhelmingly stimulated many brain cells are permanently destroyed. At birth man has several millions of brain cells, but if a brain cell is destroyed it is not replaced. Therefore every overwhelming activation by physical or psychic stimuli results in the permanent loss of a certain number of brain cells. The whole structure of the brain is altered and the action patterns formed by the environmental relations of a lifetime are changed so that normal reactions can no longer be expressed. In other words, the individual becomes permanently impaired. The woman who has seen her husband assaulted or

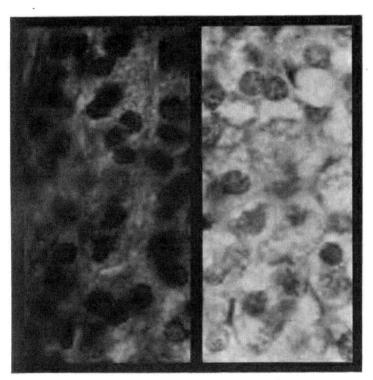

A	B
SECTION OF NORMAL ADRENAL	SECTION OF ADRENAL SHOWING EFFECT
(× 1640)	OF EXTREME EMOTION (FRIGHT)
	(× 1640)

killed, who has seen her home burned, who has seen her daughter outraged, who has seen her children starving, is herself permanently modified; she may become neurasthenic, depressed, morose, sleepless, even insane, and in any case her mechanism suffers a permanent injury.

Because of the relation between the brain and the other organs in the kinetic system, prolonged emotional stimulation results in such a steady activation of these organs — especially of the liver, the adrenals, and the thyroid, that one or another of them yields under the strain and one or another disease is established. These facts make it possible for us to understand what must have been the immediate result and to predict the remote effect of the overwhelming activations which were forced upon the Belgians.

The kinetic systems of the Belgians were activated by both contact and distance ceptor stimuli. Their contact ceptors were stimulated by bullets, by bayonets and by physical assault. Their distance ceptors were stimulated by threatening aircraft, by charging Uhlans, by the shooting and torture of relatives and friends; by the confiscation of their possessions; by the separation of families; by the

destruction of their treasures, their art, their literature, and their institutions of learning. As this stimulation was continuous, the kinetic systems of the Belgians could not be restored by adequate sleep. Later,
when they were driven out of their homes, there
was added the activation of constant homesickness.

Millions of individuals were subjected to this
vivisection, while our experiments upon animals
have been limited to a few hundred. The activation of the Belgians was continued day and night
for weeks and months, in fact will continue for
years, while our experiments on animals last but a
few hours. The subjects of our experiments have
only a few simple mechanisms. The Belgians have
the vast human endowment of a highly-developed
brain. Animals used in medical research are
anesthetized and the period of their activation
is promptly ended by death under anesthesia.
The vast majority of the Belgian people were denied
the solace of painless death, and only the surcease
which comes from exhaustion could diminish their
suffering. It should be remembered also that in
this human experiment performed by ruthless op-
erators in a country-wide laboratory, each individual was subjected to many— some to all — of

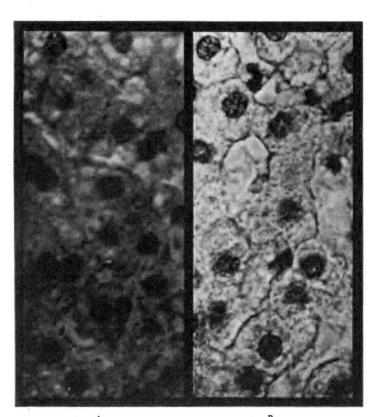

A	*B*
Section of Normal Liver (× 1640)	Section of Liver Showing Effect of Extreme Emotion (Fright) (× 1640)

the foregoing activations, while in our laboratories each animal is subjected to but one form of activation.

If our conclusions are correct, then the first effect of these stimuli upon the human organism would be a mobilization of the energizing secretions and of the energizing chemical stores in the activating glands of their bodies, — hyperchromatism of the brain cells; increased circulation of blood in the thyroid gland and increased output of thyreoiodin; an increased output of adrenalin; and an increased output of glycogen by the liver. As a consequence of this mobilization of the forces within the body, which we have compared to the mobilization of the military forces of a nation, the body would attain its maximum strength for fight or flight. As a result of the supreme effort of flight or fight or its equivalent in emotion, the alkalinity of the body fluids would be diminished and this increased acidity of the body would produce rapid respiration, rapid pulse, increased urinary output, and sweating. Cases of sudden heart failure would result from the increased blood pressure caused by the increased adrenalin output; and increased adrenalin output and acidity would cause many cases of miscarriage. In the integration for fight or flight the digestive processes would be inhibited, and among both the immediate and later results of this inhibition would be auto-intoxication and indigestion. Individuals having Bright's disease would be expected to show an increase of symptoms or would be driven to immediate renal failure, coma, and death. Individuals with cardiovascular disease would be in danger of immediate death from apoplexy.

As a result of the intensity of the activation the action patterns of the brain would be wholly disarranged. The normal action patterns of the peaceful routine of family, social, and vocational relations, heretofore balanced and even, would of necessity be dispossessed by the intense stimulation of the action patterns of fight or flight.

Since activation causes a lowering of the brain thresholds to stimuli, *neurasthenia* would result in some cases; overwhelming stimulation might cause a disastrous facilitation of response, and *insanity* would result; rupture of blood vessels in the brain would cause *paralysis;* and the destruction of a great number of brain cells as a result of exhaustion would result in permanent loss of efficiency. The increased acidity would activate the respiratory center, cause excessive sweating

A BELGIAN REFUGEE

Who lost all her possessions and witnessed the violation of her daughter.

A BELGIAN BOY

Ten years of age, whose grief and terror have made him more than once attempt suicide.

and rapid heart action, and would activate the liver.
In addition acidity would inhibit the activity of
the cerebral cortex and thus mental and muscular
power would be diminished.

One would expect the early death of those whose
margins of safety were slender, — the aged and
those having chronic diseases. As a result of the
excessive transformation of energy and the want of
rest and sleep one would expect loss in weight, and
as in cases of Graves' disease, in which the kinetic
system is subject to a continuous excessive activation, one would expect the Belgians to live years in
months, and in consequence by so much to cut off
the total number of expected years of life.

That we have not exaggerated what the protocols
of this vast experiment would lead us to expect is
proved by the evidence of many observers. There
have been many sudden deaths; many cases of
insomnia; of neurasthenia; of prostration; of
lost spirit and impaired efficiency; and generally
a loss of hope and ambition. There has been an
average loss of from six to ten pounds in weight.
Many Belgians were found dead in their beds without external injuries, and many died after a brief
illness. (A number of cases of apoplexy were seen.)

Children were prematurely born on the streets, in railway stations, or on trains. There have already been many suicides — among children as well as among adults; and children as well as adults have become insane.

It is to be expected that these conditions will continue and progress, and that there will be an increasing number of cases of Bright's disease and apoplexy. The posthumous children have been robbed of their birthright of healthy bodies and stable nervous systems. The little children whose action patterns had not been formed are the only ones who may bear their rude transplantation without loss of mental or physical efficiency. The Belgian exiles whom I have seen show a loss in morale; they are preoccupied, absent-minded, diseased, homesick, weak, dejected, bitter, and broken. They have suffered a permanent loss which is beyond compensation and beyond redemption. Thus millions of men, women, children, and unborn infants have been subjected to a vivisection of unparalleled cruelty unsurpassed in the history of man or of the lower animals. It is as if upon Belgium as a whole, every degree of physical, mental and moral torture had been inflicted *without anesthesia*. In fact, in the

FAMILY OF REFUGEES AT SAN SULPICE, PARIS

This family lived for weeks in a cellar during the bombardment of Rheims.

present condition of the Belgian exiles their progressive moral vivisection still continues.

Having interpreted the Belgian phenomena from a mechanistic viewpoint, what does the mechanistic viewpoint suggest for the future of the Belgians? Although the Belgian dead cannot be resurrected, although the lost brain cells cannot be replaced; although the damaged organs cannot be restored; although the foundations of health are permanently weakened, — a mechanistic viewpoint would suggest the mediation of the further progress of physical and moral destruction by repairing the homes and fortunes of these exiles, by reuniting their families, by giving them means for reëstablishing their universities, and by so changing the environmental mold — so altering the web of life — that their further vivisection would be diminished.

CHAPTER VI

EVOLUTION TOWARD PEACE

CHAPTER VI

Evolution toward Peace

GREAT disasters lift for a moment the veil drawn by peace and prosperity over the dangerous elements, ever-present not only in the environment of man but in his own nature as well. Occasional rumblings within Vesuvius may warn a few of the dwellers upon the mountain side of the dangerous forces beneath them; but by the multitude warnings are disregarded until the mountain discloses its nature by an overwhelming eruption. So, in times of peace man disregards the threatening evidences of his true nature which are ever-manifest in daily jealousies and competitions and in petty wars, and not till the full horror of a mighty conflict is upon him does he realize the power of his own fight-lustful nature. Now that a great war once again has drawn the veil, it is possible, if we are able to make a final analysis of what is disclosed, that we may discover the manner in which those very forces which made this war possible and inevitable may be utilized to strengthen the bonds of peace, just as natural elements once feared, even worshiped, because of their menace to man's safety, are now made subservient to his welfare.

As a result of his mastery over the forces of nature man exacts from the earth a living and a surplus. Having an excess of food, shelter, and clothing he no longer practices infanticide, — but for no better reason. Having an excess of food, shelter, and clothing, having established law and order and conventions; woman, the race breeder, the ancient cultivator of the fields; woman, the property of hunting, fighting man, has gone to school, and has begun to assist in the management of the new machinery of civilization.

When the novelty of this new estate shall have worn off, perhaps man and woman together will solve the problems of the propagation and the care of the human race as intelligently and as practically as they have worked out the problem of the propagation and the care of their domestic animals. It may be that woman's effort to secure the franchise is but the surface indication of a great biologic movement — one that women themselves do not fully understand any more than the chick struggling out of its shell understands that it is in the process of being born.

Perhaps the present feminist agitation will bring a favorable change in human destiny. When we consider that woman was evolved to preserve, to perpetuate the species; that in the course of that evolution she developed altruistic traits — traits which are the logical results of her care for her children — it would seem that there must now also be evolved within her a great fundamental reaction against the harshness of man. This harshness, this pugnacity, this greed for killing, was put into man through evolution, and it cannot be mitigated save through further evolution. Perhaps one of the influences in this further evolution will be woman's natural reaction against needless violence.

Whatever the future may bring, however, man to-day betrays at every turn that he is in reality a red-handed glutton whose phylogenetic action patterns are facilitated for the killing of his own and of other species; that with all of his beneficent control of the forces of nature, he has created also vast forces for his own destruction, so vast that civilized man is to-day in a death struggle with the Frankenstein of his own creation; that, although he controls a world of limitless force and endless machinery, he yet fails to control that all-important mechanism — himself. Can this animal, bloodthirsty by nature and training, who produces and kills millions of animals yearly and who kills at intervals hundreds of thousands of his fellow-men — can he be so modified as to live in *relative* peace? Can man in the possession of the power to create, minimize his tendency towards self-destruction?

A suggestion as to how this may be done is seen in the method by which the killing reactions are diminished in other fighting animals — animals evolved to be life destroyers even more than man. For example, the action patterns of the dog, the preservation of whose ancestors depended on their killing other animals, have been so modified by man that now the peace element in his action patterns has been augmented and his killing patterns diminished. Thus through breeding and through training has the brain of the dog been modified. If the dog, whose reactions are in comparison to those of man so few, whose brain has not acquired through phylogeny facilitated paths of action for mutual help, even for herd existence, — if the mechanism of the dog has been so successfully modified by man, what limit can be set to the modification of the action patterns of man by education and training planned for the strengthening of the action patterns of peace ?

If we have not heretofore found a means of preventing war, we have at least found that certain things cannot prevent war; we know that our present system of education cannot prevent war; we know that commercial relations, even treaties, cannot prevent war; we know that the burden of debt, bankruptcy, and the resultant grind of poverty cannot prevent war; we know that religion and military systems, and even the fear of wounds and hunger, of suffering and death, cannot prevent war; in short, the very civilization of to-day is itself at war! The civilization of to-day cannot prevent war, because under existing conditions war is inevitable; because it is the normal result of the action patterns, created by the mold in which has been formed the present generation of men.

The earliest predisposing cause of the present War of Nations was the establishment of an action pattern of war in the first child who as a man is now

H

concerned therein. *This event was a microscopic declaration of war.* Multiples of like action patterns made inevitable the final declaration of war between the nations. Therefore, like Prometheus, man is chained to the rock of fate, unless a new philosophy be introduced; unless the web of life of the majority of the inhabitants of the earth be so modified that in the next generation peace patterns shall be increased and war patterns lessened.

How may this be accomplished? An analysis of man's adaptive response to the web of life may show the way, since conduct is the result of both phylogeny (species experience) and ontogeny (individual experience).

The offspring of animals at the time of birth are slightly if at all equipped to adapt themselves to environment; the simpler the reaction of a species, the earlier is its mechanism for adaptation completed. Hence we find for the young of each species different methods and different periods of time for completing their adaptation for adult life, varying from the simple adaptation of the fish, that never even knows its parents, to the increasingly complex adaptations of the birds, whose parents protect, feed, and give them their simple training; of the beaver, whose off-

THE CHARGE

spring are taught even to play at making dams ; and finally of the gregarious animals whose young remain with the flock or herd and are taught by example. The carnivora train their young to kill, and the young of monkeys, whose survival depends upon an adaptation to continual alertness, receive from their parents a careful training in strategy. To accomplish this longer tutelage required by the anthropoids, the parents keep their offspring with them during a longer period of time, and thus is formed the family — the dawn of human society. From the periods of training and education received by the young of anthropoids we pass to the progressively longer periods required for the training of the Bushman, the cave man, the semi-civilized, and finally the civilized man.

The brain of man may be likened to a moving-picture film running from birth to death. Among the numberless pictures some obtain possession of the final common path, or become adequate stimuli. Those that become adequate stimuli produce action patterns, the responses of which to repetitions of the stimuli by which they were produced make up the conduct of the individual. In other words, man's action patterns reflect as in a mirror his environment.

If a colt grows up in the wilds, it becomes a wild horse; if bred by man, its action patterns are domestic. The young of all animals are plastic. The child of man is most plastic. If a child remain in a Christian portion of the web of life, Christian action patterns are formed; if in a pagan web, he becomes pagan; if in a peaceful web, peaceful action patterns result; if in a warlike web, warlike patterns are inevitable. The brain patterns that dominate at the close of the adolescent and at the beginning of the adult period fix and determine until death the life reactions of the individual. The action patterns thus formed in the plastic brain constitute the personality of the individual and make the reactions of the human mechanism as inevitable and as true as are the reactions of a man-made machine. A wheelbarrow cannot perform the work of an automobile, but the difference between the wheelbarrow and the automobile is less than the difference between the cannibal and the scholar.

The environment therefore is the mold which predetermines the man. If for a generation every newborn babe of China could be interchanged with every newborn babe of France, the web of life of China would create Chinese action patterns in the

THE CALL TO ARMS AND THE END RESULT

brains of the French children; and the web of life of France would create French action patterns in the brains of the Chinese children. But *relatively* China would still remain China and France would remain France. Thus if the offspring of any two alien people whose brains are comparable in size and plasticity be interchanged, the action patterns of the brains of the children will be modified, but the web of life in each nation will remain fixed. The molten metal adapts itself to the mold — the mold remains unchanged. The only way by which the action patterns of a people can be altered is by changing the mold — altering the environment. Thus slowly science and invention and human experience modify the mold which stamps generations to come.

In America the plastic newborn of many races and nationalities are gathered and are so melted and molded in our public schools that the second generation of European origin can scarcely be distinguished from those of *Mayflower* descent.

Therefore, if we desire that in our children action patterns of peace shall predominate over war patterns, the disadvantages of war as well as its advantages should be set forth in the nursery, the school, and the university; in daily papers, magazines, and books. In the web of life of childhood, as well as of maturity, the consequences of war should be as prominent as the glory of war. The thrilling departure of patriot husband or son should be paralleled by the somber desertion of wife or mother; the glory of the bayonet charge by its disembowelled victims; the report of the staff commander by that of the surgeon general; the monument to the victorious general by the rude cross on the grave of the private soldier; the brilliant uniform by the rags of poverty; the rejoicing of the victors by the enduring hate of the vanquished. The happiness and serenity of life should be contrasted with the illogical ending of life through war.

Children should be taught to regard as heroes those also who have made possible the conquest of nature through invention and discovery; those who have striven for and have achieved great ideals of government, of education, of science and of morals. Peace has as worthy heroes as has war!

When man comprehends his own mechanism, when he understands the dominating influence of his progenitors and appreciates the infinite possibilities of his training, then he may reach a grade of civilization which will enable him to invigorate

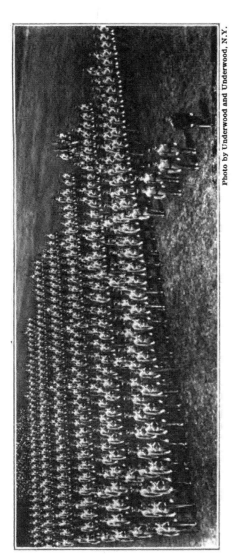

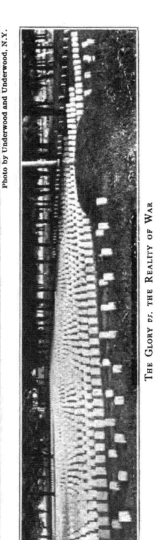

The Glory *vs.* the Reality of War

himself without ruin. Struggle is a biological necessity, and even war is preferable to pusillanimous
peace leading to degeneracy.

When the mechanistic viewpoint is generally understood, a viewpoint that fixes all responsibility
for human action here and now within one's self;
that teaches that one generation predetermines
the action of the next generation; that the newborn
infant is only the plastic clay from which the real
man is created,—a new meaning will be given to education. Then we may be intelligent enough to have
the greatest talent of the country, not at the head of
armies, or strategy boards, not in finance or industry,
but at the head of the state educational systems.
Backed by money and public opinion, a group of
supermen may evolve a system of mechanistic training which will mold the next generation into a higher
degree of adaptation to environment — an increased
fitness for service to country and to fellow-citizens.
Man at last may see that his destiny is in his own
hands and that there is no active supernatural
power that will help or hinder his career; in fact,
that his destiny in part has been determined by his
evolution — but that the balance is to be man-
made here and now.

If the human animal were under the domination of beings as superior to him, as man is superior to the domestic animals, we might expect that education would be exploited as efficiently as war has been exploited and that there might be built up a civilization freed to some extent from its menacing phylogeny.

THE SOLDIERS' BURIAL

THE following pages contain advertisements of books by the same author or on kindred subjects.

Man An Adaptive Mechanism

By GEORGE W. CRILE, M.D.

Professor of Surgery, School of Medicine, Western Reserve University ;
Visiting Surgeon to the Lakeside Hospital, Cleveland

EDITED BY ANNETTE AUSTIN, A.B.

Illustrated, Cloth, 8vo

The subject of Dr. Crile's book is an interpretation
of the phenomena of health and disease in the light
of their origin in conditions of the internal and external environment of man's body during its age-long
evolutionary struggle for adaptation to its physical
medium. It is an attempt to show that the phenomena
of pathologic processes — acute and chronic diseases
— no less than the phenomena of normal living —.
emotion, work, ambition, ideals — are the outcome of
this ancient continuous friction which has resulted,
likewise, in the evolution in the body of a system of
organs consisting of the brain, adrenal, liver, thyroid,
muscles, the function of which — coördinating in harmony or disharmony with the activating stimuli of the
environment — is to produce the adaptive responses
which are recognized now as normal processes, now
as abnormal reactions.

THE MACMILLAN COMPANY

Publishers   64-66 Fifth Avenue   New York

The Pentecost of Calamity

By OWEN WISTER
Author of " The Virginian," etc.

Boards, 16mo, 50 cents

The author of "The Virginian" has written a new book which describes, more forcibly and clearly than any other account so far published, the meaning, to America, of the tragic changes which are taking place in the hearts and minds of the German people.

Written with ease and charm of style, it is prose that holds the reader for its very beauty, even as it impresses him with its force. It is doubtful whether there will come out of the entire mass of war literature a more understanding or suggestive survey.

"Owen Wister has depicted the tragedy of Germany and has hinted at the possible tragedy of the United States. . . . We wish it could be read in full by every American."
— *The Outlook.*

The Military Unpreparedness of the United States
By FREDERIC L. HUIDEKOPER

Cloth, 8vo

By many army officers the author of this work is regarded as the foremost military expert in the United States. For nine years he has been striving to awaken the American people to a knowledge of the weaknesses of their land forces and the defencelessness of the country. Out of his extensive study and research he has compiled the present volume, which represents the last word on this subject. It comes at a time when its importance cannot be overestimated, and in the eight hundred odd pages given over to the discussion there are presented facts and arguments with which every citizen should be familiar. Mr. Huidekoper's writings in this field are already well known. These hitherto, however, have been largely confined to magazines and pamphlets, but his book deals with the matters under consideration with that frankness and authority evidenced in these previous contributions and much more comprehensively.

THE MACMILLAN COMPANY
Publishers   64-66 Fifth Avenue   New York

The World War:

How it Looks to the Nations Involved and What it Means to Us

By ELBERT FRANCIS BALDWIN

Decorated cloth, 12mo, $1.25

The present war in Europe has called forth a great many books bearing on its different phases, but in the majority of instances these have been written from the standpoint of some one of the nations. Elbert Francis Baldwin has here, however, brought together within the compass of a single volume a survey of the entire field.

Mr. Baldwin was in Europe at the outbreak of hostilities. He mingled with the people, observing their spirit and temper more intimately than it has been permitted most writers to do, and in consequence the descriptions which he gives of the German, or French, or English, or Russian attitude are truer and more complete than those found in previous studies of the war.

A Journal of Impressions in Belgium

By MAY SINCLAIR

Cloth, 12mo, $1.50

May Sinclair is the latest English author who has written a book as the outgrowth of the war, and a most unusual and fascinating book it is, too. It is entitled "A Journal of Impressions in Belgium" and records the mental effect produced by the war upon the distinguished novelist when she went to the front with an ambulance corps. The journal cannot properly be termed a war book; it is, rather, a May Sinclair book in that it deals with her reaction to the fighting and the experiences through which she passed, and not with the military or technical side of the engagements. It is perhaps as graphic a picture as has yet come to America from the war zone.

THE MACMILLAN COMPANY

Publishers   64-66 Fifth Avenue   New York

Russia and the World

By STEPHEN GRAHAM

Author of " With the Russian Pilgrims to Jerusalem," " With Poor Immigrants to America," etc.

Illustrated, cloth, 8vo, $2.00

At the outbreak of the present European war Mr. Graham was in Russia, and his book opens, therefore, with a description of the way the news of war was received on the Chinese frontier, one thousand miles from a railway station, where he happened to be when the Tsar's summons came. Following this come other chapters on Russia and the War, considering such questions as, Is It a Last War ?, Why Russia is Fighting, The Economic Isolation of Russia, An Aeroplane Hunt at Warsaw, Suffering Poland : A Belgium of the East, and The Soldier and the Cross.

" It shows the author creeping as near as he was allowed to the firing line. It gives broad views of difficult questions, like the future of the Poles and the Jews. It rises into high politics, forecasts the terms of peace and the rearrangement of the world, east and west, that may follow. But the salient thing in it is its interpretation for Western minds of the spirit of Russia." — *London Times.*

German World Policies

(Der Deutsche Gedanke in der Welt)

By PAUL ROHRBACH

Translated by DR. EDMUND VON MACH

Cloth, 12mo, $1.25

Paul Rohrbach has been for several years the most popular author of books on politics and economics in Germany. He is described by his translator as a " constructive optimist," one who, at the same time, is an incisive critic of those shortcomings which have kept Germany, as he thinks, from playing the great part to which she is called. In this volume Dr. Rohrbach gives a true insight into the character of the German people, their aims, fears, and aspirations.

" Dr. von Mach renders an extraordinary service to his country in making known to English readers at this time a book like Rohrbach's."
— *New York Globe.*

" A clear insight into Prussian ideals." — *Boston Transcript.*

" A valuable, significant, and most informing book."
— *New York Tribune.*

THE MACMILLAN COMPANY

Publishers   64-66 Fifth Avenue   New York

With the Russian Army

By Col. ROBERT McCORMICK

Illustrated, 8vo., $2.00

This book deals with the author's experiences in the war area. The work traces the cause of the war from the treaty of 1878 through the Balkan situation. It contains many facts drawn from personal observation, for Col. McCormick has had opportunities such as have been given to no other man during the present engagements. He has been at the various headquarters and actually in the trenches. One of the most interesting chapters of the volume is the concluding one dealing with great personalities of the war from first-hand acquaintance.

The work contains a considerable amount of material calculated to upset generally accepted ideas, comparisons of the fighting forces, and much else that is fresh and original.

THE MACMILLAN COMPANY

Publishers 64-66 Fifth Avenue New York

www.ingramcontent.com/pod-product-compliance
Lightning Source LLC
LaVergne TN
LVHW012203040326
832903LV00003B/82